DATE DUE

American Symbols
AND THEIR Meanings

ROCK 'N' ROLL

American Symbols
AND THEIR Meanings

THE ALAMO

THE AMERICAN FLAG

THE BALD EAGLE

THE CONFEDERATE FLAG

THE CONSTITUTION

THE DECLARATION OF INDEPENDENCE

ELLIS ISLAND

INDEPENDENCE HALL

THE JEFFERSON MEMORIAL

THE LIBERTY BELL

THE LINCOLN MEMORIAL

MOUNT RUSHMORE

THE NATIONAL ANTHEM

THE PLEDGE OF ALLEGIANCE

ROCK 'N' ROLL

THE STATUE OF LIBERTY

UNCLE SAM

VIETNAM VETERANS MEMORIAL

THE WASHINGTON MONUMENT

THE WHITE HOUSE

ROCK 'N' ROLL

HAL MARCOVITZ

MASON CREST PUBLISHERS
PHILADELPHIA

First printing

1 3 5 7 9 8 6 4 2

Library of Congress Cataloging-in-Publication Data on file at the Library of Congress

ISBN 1-59084-036-4

Publisher's note: all quotations in this book come from original sources, and contain the spelling and grammatical inconsistencies of the original text.

American Symbols AND THEIR Meanings

CONTENTS

THE IMPORTANCE OF AMERICAN SYMBOLS

Symbols are not merely ornaments to admire—they also tell us stories. If you look at one of them closely, you may want to find out why it was made and what it truly means. If you ask people who live in the society in which the symbol exists, you will learn some things. But by studying the people who created that symbol and the reasons why they made it, you will understand the deepest meanings of that symbol.

The United States owes its identity to great events in history, and the most remarkable American Symbols are rooted in these events. The struggle for independence from Great Britain gave America the Declaration of Independence, the Liberty Bell, the American flag, and other images of freedom. The War of 1812 gave the young country a song dedicated to the flag, "The Star-Spangled Banner," which became our national anthem. Nature gave the country its national animal, the bald eagle. These symbols established the identity of the new nation, and set it apart from the nations of the Old World.

To be emotionally moving, a symbol must strike people with a sense of power and unity. But it often takes a long time for a new symbol to be accepted by all the people, especially if there are older symbols that have gradually lost popularity. For example, the image of Uncle Sam has replaced Brother Jonathan, an earlier representation of the national will, while the Statue of Liberty has replaced Columbia, a woman who represented liberty to Americans in the early 19th century. Since then, Uncle Sam and the Statue of Liberty have endured and have become cherished icons of America.

Of all the symbols, the Statue of Liberty has perhaps the most curious story, for unlike other symbols, Americans did not create her. She was created by the French, who then gave her to America. Hence, she represented not what Americans thought of their country but rather what the French thought of America. It was many years before Americans decided to accept this French goddess of Liberty as a symbol for the United States and its special role among the nations: to spread freedom and enlighten the world.

This series of books is valuable because it presents the story of each of America's great symbols in a freshly written way and will contribute to the students' knowledge and awareness of them. It is to be hoped that this information will awaken an abiding interest in American history, as well as in the meanings of American symbols.

—*Barry Moreno,*
librarian and historian
Ellis Island/Statue of Liberty National Monument

Guitarist Les Paul, outlined in the red glow of stage lights, jams at a show in 2001. In the summer of 1929, Paul figured out how to amplify the sound of his guitar strings, creating the electric guitar. His invention would revolutionize popular music in the 1950s, leading to a new form of music known as rock 'n' roll.

RED HOT RED

As a young boy growing up in Waukesha, Wisconsin, Lester William Polfuss often annoyed his parents and friends with constant and endless questions about how things worked. It seemed the boy was most curious about radios, telephones, and other household electrical devices.

As Lester devoted many hours at home to tinkering with radios, he started listening more and more to the programs broadcast over the *airwaves*. He grew increasingly interested in the guitar players he heard on the radio, and decided to learn how to play the instrument himself. He had been taking piano lessons for some time

Although stringed instruments date back at least 4,000 years, the first modern acoustic guitar was fashioned in Spain in 1850 by Antonio de Torres Jurado.

and was considered a talented musician. Lester had perfect pitch—he could hear a song once, recognize the notes, and be able to play it back with little or no practice.

Lester bought his first guitar for $2.49, and he had one brief lesson. A guitar player named "Pie Plant Pete" Moye had his own radio show broadcast out of Chicago, Illinois, and toured many of the small cities in the Midwest performing shows in theaters. At a show in Waukesha, Lester talked his way backstage and met Pete, who was touched by the boy's enthusiasm for the guitar. Pete showed Lester how to play a few chords and sketched out some lessons on a piece of paper, showing Lester where to place his fingers on the neck of the instrument.

"He took that piece of paper home with him and within a few days I received a letter from his mom saying she had purchased him a Sears, Roebuck guitar," Moye later wrote. "Well sir, every time we would be within 50 to 100 miles of Waukesha, here would come Mrs. Polfuss and her boy. And each time she would insist on my hearing how he had progressed on guitar. In only a month or two he had surpassed my guitar playing by a country mile."

As he grew older, Lester started performing himself.

By the time he was 14, Lester Polfuss was tall and skinny with big ears, a broad smile and a shock of red hair. Around Waukesha, he became known as "Red Hot Red."

By now, he had also learned the harmonica and was performing at church socials, fraternal organization meetings, cafes, and *speakeasies*. He also brought along an old steel washtub, which he turned over and kicked with his boot. That was the drum for his one-man band.

In the summer of 1929, Lester found his talents in demand at Beekman's barbecue stand in nearby Goerke's Corners. Beekman's had no tables—just a large parking lot where guests ate in their cars. With cars driving in and out, and waitresses clanging by with trays of food, Lester often found himself trying to sing over a great deal of noise. One night he brought along an old microphone, wired it into a radio speaker, and was able to *amplify* his voice and harmonica over the racket in the parking lot.

But Lester's *acoustic* guitar couldn't be heard above the din in the parking lot. So Lester "borrowed" a combination radio-phonograph player owned by his father. He took the needle from the phonograph arm and stuck it into the wood below the strings, so it would "pick up" the vibrations when he played the notes. Then, he ran a wire from the needle through the speakers of the

> The first song recorded on a phonograph was "Mary Had a Little Lamb" by the inventor of the device, Thomas Edison.

Les Paul is one of the godfathers of rock 'n' roll music, but as a musician he had little to do with perfecting the sound that would dominate the music scene during the 1950s. Instead, Paul played jazz, blues, and popular tunes. These were appreciated more by the parents of teenagers than their sons and daughters.

Nevertheless, Paul's contribution to rock music can be traced to his innovations in guitar playing and his interest in developing the guitar as an important musical instrument. His designs for solid-body electric guitars prompted the Gibson Guitar Company to start manu-facturing electric guitars in 1951, and the company continues to manufacture a series of guitars it calls "Les Paul guitars."

He also helped launch "multi-track" recording—the technique used by engineers to record many parts played by the same musician, then merge them into the song during the production process. His 1948 song "Brazil" featured six guitar parts, all played by Paul.

In the meantime, he had many successes as a record-ing artist. His two No. 1 hits were "How High the Moon" and "Vaya Con Dios." He decided to retire in the 1960s, but has never managed to stay retired. He is constantly called on to perform on television specials and music festivals around the world.

radio. He cranked up the volume as high as it would go and strummed the strings. It worked: the needle heard the notes and amplified them through the radio speaker. Now, folks all over Beekman's parking lot would be able to hear the music.

Lester Polfuss had just made the first electric guitar. The phonograph needle had served as the "pick-up," the key part of the electric guitar that transfers the sound from the strings to the electric amplifier. It was crude, but the principle behind what Lester had done would be copied by guitar makers in years to come. The instrument would dominate rock 'n' roll music in America.

Even Lester knew he was on to something big. The first night he tried out the contraption at Beekman's, his tips tripled. Said Lester: "The electric guitar spelled money."

Lester soon dropped the name Red Hot Red and became known as Les Paul, forging a career as a singing and recording artist. But he always found time to tinker with guitars and electrical equipment, looking for ways to make a true electric guitar. When he first brought his ideas for a solid-body electric guitar to the Gibson Guitar Company, the company didn't see the need.

"They politely ushered me out the door," Paul recalled. "They called it the broomstick with the pick-up on it."

But in 1951, on the eve of the explosion of rock 'n' roll music, Gibson changed its mind and put its engineers to work perfecting a solid-body electric guitar—a design that is still in use today. Ted McCarty, the president of Gibson, convinced Paul to lend his name to the new instrument. Today, many Gibson electric guitars are known as "Les Paul guitars."

Said Ralph Gleason, a noted music critic: "No one in the history of pop music has had a greater effect on the ultimate pop sound than Les Paul."

Elvis Presley swivels his hips before an adoring crowd of teenage girls. Elvis, who has been nicknamed the King of Rock 'n' Roll, would become the biggest star of the 1950s. More than 25 years after his death in 1977, Elvis remains an icon of American pop culture.

HELL BREAKS LOOSE

*I*t didn't take long for the Gibson Company's electric guitars to find their way into the hands of musicians anxious to start playing the new music known as "rock 'n' roll."

The sound was a *hodgepodge* of a number of musical styles. The early rockers borrowed their sounds from the black *rhythm* and *blues* and gospel singers, added the dance beat of the 1940s swing bands, and sprinkled in the *riffs* played by the country and western musicians. The energy of the music was high and the *vocals* loud. The sound soon took on a life of its own.

Across America, radio stations—anxious to develop

audiences among the nation's growing population of teenagers—started paying attention to the type of music kids seemed to like. At radio station WJW in Cleveland, Ohio, disc jockey Alan Freed was hired in 1951 to play classical music—the works of such masters as Beethoven, Bach, and Mozart. Freed soon realized rock 'n' roll had captured the ears of young people.

"I went to the station manager and talked him into permitting me to follow my classical program with a rock 'n' roll party," Freed said.

Freed named his show *The Moon Dog Rock 'n' Roll House Party*, picking as the show's theme the song "Blues for Moondog," a song by early rocker Todd Rhodes.

Freed is, in fact, credited by many people with the term "rock 'n' roll." Back in 1934, though, songwriter Richard Whiting, who wrote such standards as "Hooray for Hollywood" and "Ain't We Got Fun," penned a composition titled "Rock and Roll." Whatever the origins of the name, *The Moon Dog Rock 'n' Roll House Party* soon became one of the most popular radio shows in Cleveland.

Meanwhile, a former country and western singer named Bill Haley and his band, the Comets, recorded a song titled "Rock Around the Clock." In 1955, the song was included in the soundtrack for the movie *Blackboard Jungle*, a film that told the story of young and angry teenagers. The movie captured the spirit of the nation's teens, who rebelled against the authority of their parents and teachers, and the song shot to the top of the record sales charts.

In the South around this time, a new sound that was called "rockabilly" had captured the attention of young

Alan Freed was born near Johnstown, Pennsylvania, on December 21, 1921. His ambition was to become a professional musician and band-leader, but an ear infection ended that possibility. Instead, Freed developed an interest in radio, and after college landed jobs at small stations in Ohio and western Pennsylvania.

In 1951, Freed joined WJW in Cleveland. He soon realized that local teenagers were big fans of a new type of loud, fast-paced music, and he talked station executives into letting him have a show devoted to this sound. Although the term "rock 'n' roll" had been in use for a number of years, Freed is believed to be the first to apply it to the new sound.

After spinning records in Cleveland and staging a number of successful rock 'n' roll concerts, Freed took a job at radio station WINS in New York, where his career took off. By the late 1950s, Freed was the most important voice of rock 'n' roll in America.

Freed's luck would not hold out. In 1960, he was charged by federal authorities with evading income taxes. He was accused of taking money from record promoters to play their songs on the air and not paying taxes on the income. The incident became known as the "Payola Scandal," and it ended Alan Freed's career. He died in 1965 in Palm Springs, California, at the age of 43, penniless and a broken man.

listeners. There was no question that rockabilly was rock 'n' roll, but this form of the music contained a heavy dose of the hillbilly country and western sound. Singers such as Buddy Holly, Carl Perkins, Roy Orbison, and Jerry Lee Lewis became big rockabilly stars.

In Memphis, Tennessee, a major producer of the rockabilly sound was Sun Records, founded by Sam Phillips. Phillips was a former disc jockey and radio engineer. He built his own recording studio and intended to make records of black rhythm and blues singers, whose music he loved. In the South, because of racism, black artists often could not find record companies willing to make their records.

But by the early 1950s, business was poor and Phillips decided to search for a new sound. In 1953, a young truck driver from Tupelo, Mississippi, wandered into the Sun Records studio. He paid $4 to make a record as a gift for his mother. A few months later, he returned to record two more songs. Phillips liked the recordings, so he called the young man, whose name was Elvis Presley, and asked him to come back to the studio and record a few more songs.

Presley cut the song "Red Hot and Blue" for Sun Records. On July 10, 1954, the Memphis disc jockey Dewey Phillips played the song on his WHBQ radio show. "Dewey played that thing," said Sam Phillips, "and the phones started ringing. Honey, I'll tell you, all hell broke loose."

Within 10 days, Sun Records sold 5,000 copies of "Red Hot and Blue," and the song quickly became the top-selling single in Memphis record stores. It didn't take long for teenagers, particularly girls, to discover Presley's talent, charm, good looks and unique brand of rockabilly music. He wore tight pants, black shirts with

Four music legends in the studio at Sun Records in Memphis, Tennessee: Elvis Presley is seated, and behind him are Johnny Cash, Carl Perkins, and Jerry Lee Lewis. This photo was taken in 1955.

the collars turned up, and no tie. His hair was a bit longer than what adults were used to seeing, and greased into a wild *pompadour* style. What's more, he brought a raw energy to his performances. He swaggered on stage, grasping the microphone as though he intended to rip it from its post.

Eventually, he signed with bigger record companies, which were able to promote and market his music nationwide. In 1956, his single "Heartbreak Hotel" became the top-selling record in the country. It was the first of Presley's five hits in 1956. On September 9, 1956, the nation's adults learned what their sons and daughters already knew. That night, on the *Ed Sullivan Show*, Elvis performed four songs and created a national scandal when he swiveled his hips suggestively.

Two of the most important entertainers of the 1950s showcased rock 'n' roll artists on their popular television programs: Ed Sullivan (left) and *American Bandstand* host Dick Clark (right).

Many adults, particularly the entertainment critics, didn't know what to make of it all. But Ed Sullivan and his producers knew a talent when they saw one, and Elvis was invited back two more times. In later appearances on the popular TV show, the cameraman was told to shoot Elvis from the waist up.

Television became very important to rock 'n' roll in the 1960s. The medium was just coming into its own as the premier mode of entertainment in America. Although the *Ed Sullivan Show* continued to be popular, the program was aimed at an older audience, and only occasionally featured rock 'n' roll acts. Many local TV stations produced their own rock 'n' roll shows. One such show was *Bandstand*, which premiered in 1952 on TV station WFIL in Philadelphia. On August 5, 1957, the show was renamed *American Bandstand* and broadcast on 67 stations coast to coast. The host was Dick Clark, who for 90 minutes each afternoon featured top American rock 'n' roll acts as well as a studio dance floor filled with teenagers gyrating on camera to the music.

> **Dick Clark admitted to being totally ignorant of rock 'n' roll when he agreed to take over the *Bandstand* program in 1956. He confessed to a record promoter: "I don't understand this music."**

It was all clean, wholesome fun. Within a year of its debut, 40 million kids a day hurried home after school to turn on *American Bandstand*.

The unique sound of rock 'n' roll underwent many changes during the 1960s. The American sound had crossed the water to Europe, and in Great Britain many young musicians began playing their own variations of songs by Chuck Berry, B.B. King, Little Richard, and other early rock 'n' roll stars. Among these British rockers were four young men who would change the music world: the Beatles.

ROCK 'N' ROLL EVOLVES

*N*early eight years after Elvis Presley swiveled his hips on the *Ed Sullivan Show*, the popular Sunday night program introduced another major rock 'n' roll act to the American people.

Four young men from Liverpool, England, who had become a sensation in Europe, crossed the Atlantic Ocean, betting that American teenagers would enjoy their rollicking electric sound. On the night of February 9, 1964, the Beatles performed on the Sullivan show.

Some months before, Sullivan had been traveling in England when he witnessed 15,000 screaming fans descend on a London airport terminal, delaying flights while they swarmed around the four musicians: John Lennon, Paul McCartney, George Harrison, and Ringo Starr.

"I made up my mind that this was the same sort of mass *hysteria* that had characterized the Elvis Presley days," Sullivan said. Quickly, he booked the group for an appearance on his TV show.

On the night of the Beatles' appearance on the Sullivan show, 728 wild teenagers—most of them girls—jammed the theater seats. When Sullivan took the stage and uttered the now-famous words—"And now, the Beatles!"—the place erupted. As the four lads belted out the lyrics to "All My Loving" the girls screamed, pulled their hair, fainted, and bounced out of their seats seemingly out of control. At home, more than 73 million people had tuned in. Adults were shocked. But the kids knew what it was all about.

The appearance of the Beatles on the Sullivan show marked the beginning of what became known as the "British Invasion"—the immense popularity of English rock 'n' roll groups in America. Although none of them would ever prove to be as popular as the Beatles, many came close. The Rolling Stones and their lead singer, Mick Jagger, created such rock *anthems* as "Satisfaction" and "Jumpin' Jack Flash."

John Lennon was so nervous about the Beatles' first performance on the *Ed Sullivan Show* that he taped the lyrics to the group's songs to the back of his guitar.

The Beach Boys were one of the most popular American groups of the early 1960s because of their upbeat, fun-loving sound. Their lives did not always reflect this easy-going ideal, however. Singer/songwriter Brian Wilson (right) was obsessed with achieving the pop success of the Beatles. He eventually suffered a mental breakdown.

The Stones had a *raunchy*, bad boy image. Other British bands were less offensive. Groups like Herman's Hermits and the Dave Clark Five produced hits that were good-natured and fun to hear.

British stars weren't the only ones cutting records. Indeed, there were popular American groups that were creating distinctive sounds as well.

Berry Gordy (inset) was the founder of Motown Records in Detroit. Soon the small record label had some of the most popular musicians in America, including the Supremes (top), as well as Smokey Robinson and the Miracles, The Temptations, and The Four Tops. Their uniquely American music became known as the Motown Sound.

The Beach Boys were among the first groups to popularize the California surf sound, singing about lazy days on the beach with nothing more to do than wax their surfboards, work on their tans, and watch the girls go by. In Hollywood, the series of "Beach Party" movies featuring teen sensations Frankie Avalon and Annette Funicello proved to be enormously popular; they featured goofy plots, girls in bikinis and lots of beach music. In 1963, the group Surfaris recorded "Wipe Out," a major instrumental hit that showed just how dominant the electric guitar had become in rock 'n' roll music.

Another truly American sound came out of Detroit, Michigan, where a young black record producer named Berry Gordy founded Motown, a record company that specialized in promoting black talent.

Motown was started in 1959 with a $700 investment that Gordy borrowed from his sister. He used the money to rent and renovate a house in Detroit he equipped with a recording studio. Motown had its first minor hit that September, when Smokey Robinson and the Miracles recorded "Bad Girl." The song made the top 100 on the national pop charts. A year later, Smokey and his group had an even bigger hit with the single "Shop Around," and in 1961 the Marvelettes' song "Please Mr. Postman" hit No. 1. Motown was on its way.

The Motown sound was heavy on rhythm and vocals and had a lively beat. During the 1960s, Motown was responsible for launching the careers of such black artists as the Supremes, Temptations, Stevie Wonder, and the Four Tops. In 1966, 75 percent of all songs released by Motown hit the charts as top-sellers.

Late in the 1960s, new sounds started dominating rock 'n' roll. Many of the rock stars of the era had discovered drugs, and were openly using them and letting the substances influence their music. It was the era of *"psychedelic* rock," featuring long and loud instrumental riffs and lyrics that glorified the effects of drug use.

The music was also known as "acid rock" after the nickname of the psychedelic drug known as *LSD.* Important groups from this era included the Grateful Dead and Jefferson Airplane, both of which got their starts in the Haight-Ashbury district of San Francisco, California.

Sadly, several psychedelic rock stars died from drug abuse, among them the singers Jim Morrison and Janis Joplin and guitar player Jimi Hendrix.

But there was no question that psychedelic music left its imprint on pop culture. Boys grew their hair long and stopped shaving. Clothes featured wild and colorful patterns. Kids went barefoot, stopped bathing, and talked a lot about "flower power." The peace sign became a

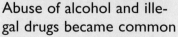

Abuse of alcohol and illegal drugs became common among rock musicians during the late 1960s. This led to the early deaths of three of rock's most promising stars: Janis Joplin, Jim Morrison, and Jimi Hendrix.

familiar symbol in America, owing to the opposition of rock stars and their fans to the war in Vietnam.

By the 1970s, things were a lot calmer, and so was the music. Rock 'n' roll artists returned to their old standbys: Boy-and-girl relationships and how to have fun on Saturday nights. In 1977, TV actor John Travolta starred in the movie *Saturday Night Fever*, which told the story of a restless paint store clerk who leaves his boring life behind on Saturday nights by donning white suits, tight shirts and gold jewelry to become a master of the disco dance floor. *Saturday Night Fever* eventually grossed more than $142 million at the box office. The film featured the music of several disco stars but particularly the brothers Barry, Robin, and Maurice Gibb, known to their fans as the Bee Gees. Within a year, the soundtrack from the film sold 30 million copies. Disco was fun, upbeat music that made people want to dance.

Meanwhile, popular music continued to evolve in different directions. The rock 'n' roll sound became harder and heavier with the success of such groups as Led Zepplin and Aerosmith. Meanwhile, a new sound, "punk rock," was emerging in urban areas. Punk rock was violent music that opposed all forms of authority. Though bands like the Sex Pistols and the Clash had some success, the punk rock movement had pretty much burned itself out by the mid-1980s.

Eddie Vedder, lead singer of the grunge band Pearl Jam, performs onstage. Pearl Jam was one of the forerunners of Seattle's grunge sound, and one of the most popular bands of the late 1980s and 1990s.

"I WANT MY MTV!"

he Buggles were a band from England that had a brief life on the popular music scene. The group played what was known as "synth-pop" music, songs that relied on the vibrating sounds made by the *synthesizer*—an electronic device that can create a variety of artificial sounds. The group formed in 1979 but within three years the Buggles had broken up, its members joining other bands.

Nevertheless, the Buggles were around long enough to make rock 'n' roll history. The group was one of the first rock 'n' roll bands to produce videos for its music. On August 1, 1981, the video of the Buggles' song,

This picture was taken from an early promotional ad for the fledgling MTV network. MTV established its popularity with teenagers and young adults by offering entertainment that changed with, and eventually shaped, trends.

"Video Killed the Radio Star," became the first video broadcast on a new cable television network known as MTV.

Music Television was born. The aim of the network, which became known as MTV, was to feature music videos—rock 'n' roll music played over dramatizations of the songs, usually acted out by the band members as well as a supporting cast of dancers.

The first head of MTV was Robert Pittman, who declared the new network would seek an audience of people under the age of 25. He told reporters he was after "TV babies"—people who seldom read newspapers or books. In the first ad campaign for MTV, viewers demanded "I want my MTV!"

Nobody understood the relationship between music and video better than Michael Jackson, a dazzling singer discovered by Berry Gordy in 1967. At the time, he was part of an act with his brothers known as the Jackson 5. By the early 1980s, although Michael still performed with his brothers, he had a successful solo career.

In 1982, Michael Jackson recorded the album *Thriller*. The record took off like a rocket and never seemed to

Michael Jackson, considered the King of Pop, got his start in music at an early age. In 1982, he released *Thriller*, which soon became one of the best selling albums of all time. Part of Jackson's success was due to the videos of his music shown on MTV.

land. Within two years, it sold a stunning 40 million copies, and nine out of its 10 songs made the Top Ten charts.

Certainly, what helped sell *Thriller* were the videos that starred Jackson singing and dancing to the songs from the album, which were played over and over again on MTV. Jackson's talents translated well to the screen: he was an electrifying dancer—his "moonwalk" was a national sensation—whose stage presence dominated each scene of the videos. What's more, the videos themselves were now regarded as an art form that attracted better directing talent. The video for the title song of *Thriller*, a musical spoof on old-time horror movies, was directed by the Hollywood director John Landis.

> **Music first became available on compact discs in 1983; soon, the format would replace vinyl records and eventually, cassette tapes.**

It was a lot of fun watching Michael Jackson moonwalk across the MTV screen, just as it had been fun 20 years before watching Frankie and Annette frolic in the surf in the "Beach Party" movies. But music had gotten very serious after those happy days at the beach, and it was about to get very serious again. Two very different types of music—one born on the hard urban streets of New

> **The first juke box was manufactured in 1906 by the Chicago Automatic Machine and Tool Company.**

York, the other in the trendy coffee bars of Seattle—were about to explode on the American music scene.

> Elton John's musical tribute to the late Princess Diana of England, "Candle in the Wind," sold 32 million copies in 37 days

In the early 1970s, a disc jockey from Jamaica known to his fans as Kool Herc started entertaining at clubs and parties in the Bronx, New York. Back in Jamaica, Kool Herc had incorporated fast-paced rhymes into his introductions to the *reggae* records he played. But reggae music did not find a wide audience in New York, so Kool Herc adapted his style to the instrumental sections of rock 'n' roll songs. Soon, Kool Herc's fans were more interested in his rhymes—which they called his raps—than with the songs he played. Kool Herc re-recorded the instrumental sections so he could extend those portions of the songs indefinitely, which gave him more time to rap over the music. This technique is called looping.

By the 1980s, rap—sometimes known as hip-hop—had a beat all its own. And rap singers used their urban, life-on-the-streets experiences to draw inspiration for their lyrics.

These singers had often grown up amid violence, drug use and other ills of inner-city life, and even though many of them became wealthy recording stars, they often found it difficult to step away from their old lifestyles.

Snoop Doggy Dogg was one of the most popular rap artists of the 1990s. He is shown here after receiving an award in 1994. Rap music was rooted in the poverty of inner-city neighbor-hoods during the late 1970s and early 1980s. It has since become a popular form of musical expression.

The early 1990s brought about a style of music called "gangsta rap," in which performers' lyrics told of the day-to-day brutality of the urban culture they came from. The shooting deaths of stars such as Tupac Shakur and Christopher Wallace (also known as the Notorious B.I.G.) show that the line between gangster and gangsta rapper is a thin one.

An alternate—but no less serious—form of rock music emerged in the 1990s. This new style of rock 'n' roll from Seattle was called "grunge" music; partly because the musicians dressed in grungy clothes—torn and faded blue jeans, old T-shirts and sweatshirts, dirty sneakers—and partly because the message in the music was sad, offering little hope for a rosy future. Grunge fans were members of "Generation X," people mostly in their teens and 20s who were born and raised during times of high unemployment.

A lot of that was reflected in the music of the top grunge bands—Nirvana, Soundgarden, Alice in Chains, and Pearl Jam, among others. On the Nirvana album *Nevermind*, the songs contained such lyrics as "I'm so ugly," "She's just as bored as me" and "I feel stupid, and contagious."

The disillusionment of most grunge bands was not just a way to sell records to jaded young people. Unfortunately, the negative attitudes prevalent in the music took their toll. Kurt Cobain, the lead singer of Nirvana, attempted suicide through a drug overdose in 1994. A few months later he succeeded, this time using a shotgun. The tragedy of his unnecessary death caused music lovers to rethink the grim outlook of grunge.

In August 1969, hundreds of thousands of people hike to a small farm in upstate New York, where many of the best rock musicians of the day were scheduled to perform. The Woodstock Music Festival—dubbed "four days of peace and love"—is one of the most famous music festivals.

ROCK MUSIC'S ULTIMATE ACT

"The times," Bob Dylan once sang, "they are a-changin'." The folk singer from Hibbing, Minnesota, meant that by the 1960s, young people had come into their own and were prepared to lead society into a series of dramatic social changes. Dylan would help provide the musical inspiration for them.

As a young boy, Robert Zimmerman was devoted to blues music, listening to such masters as Muddy Waters and John Lee Hooker. But like most teenagers in the 1950s, he was drawn to rock 'n' roll. He was already an accomplished guitar player by his freshman year in high school. By 1959, though, he had discovered folk music and started playing in the coffeehouses in Minneapolis frequented by students at the University of Minnesota. Two years later, he was in Greenwich Village, using the name Bob Dylan. He drew his new name from Dylan Thomas, a poet whom he admired.

In 1963, Dylan released the album *Freewheelin'*, which featured the single "Blowin' in the Wind." The song became an anthem for a growing movement for social change in America. Other songs of protest followed. Soon, many singers were voicing their concerns about the problems of American society. In many cases, their words were aimed at the unpopular war in Vietnam.

In August 1969, with the war in Vietnam at the height of its intensity, rock promoters John Roberts and Joel Rosenman planned a three-day concert near Woodstock, New York. And while music was supposed to be the main attraction of the festival, it was clear that music of protest would be what concertgoers would hear from the stage. Indeed, Roberts and Rosenman billed the Woodstock Rock Festival as "Three Days of Peace and Music."

There had been outdoor rock festivals before. In January 1967, some 50,000 people attended the Monterey Pop Festival in California. But no one was prepared for the massive crowds that showed up at Woodstock. More than 400,000 people found their way to Max Yasgur's farm in Bethel, the site of the festival. And there was no question, the message throughout the crowd was the same message heard from the stage and the towering sound speakers.

Certainly, music as a vehicle for social change didn't end when the troops left Vietnam in 1973. In 1985, stadiums in London, England, and Philadelphia, Pennsylvania, filled to overflowing capacity for the Live-Aid concerts, rock 'n' roll festivals organized by the Irish rocker Bob Geldof to help raise money to feed famine victims in Africa. The concerts and subsequent sales of the Live-Aid records raised some $70 million for the effort.

"To get the greatest pop musicians and get them to play their music live to the world, surely that is the ultimate act pop music can do," Geldof said.

Other rock stars have embraced similar causes. For example, Sting, the former lead singer of the Police, has dedicated his life to preserving the Amazon rain forests, a precious natural resource that is being destroyed by the development of South American cities. And in September 2001, such music stars as Bruce Springsteen, U2, and Neil Young joined with other rock artists and actors in a television concert to benefit victims of the September 11 terrorist attack on the World Trade Center in New York City and the Pentagon in Washington, D.C.

Since the days when Alan Freed started spinning platters on a Cleveland radio station, the American form of music known as rock 'n' roll has influenced, and been embraced by, audiences across the globe.

1929 Lester Polfuss, soon to be known as Les Paul, fastens a phonograph needle to his acoustic guitar and wires it to a radio speaker, making the first crude electric guitar.

1947 Bell Laboratories develops the transistor.

1951 Gibson Guitar Company begins work on the first solid-body electric guitar; Cleveland, Ohio, disc jockey Alan Freed launches *The Moon Dog Rock 'n' Roll House Party* on radio station WJW.

1954 Bill Haley and the Comets record "Rock Around the Clock"; on July 10, Memphis, Tennessee, disc jockey Dewey Phillips plays "Red Hot and Blue" by Elvis Presley.

1956 Elvis Presley performs on the Ed Sullivan Show on September 9.

1957 American Bandstand premiers on 67 TV stations in America in August 5.

1959 Berry Gordy founds the record company Motown in Detroit, Michigan.

1963 Bob Dylan records "Blowin' in the Wind." The song becomes the anthem for the civil rights movement.

1964 The Beatles perform on the Ed Sullivan Show on February 9.

1967 The Beatles release *Sgt. Pepper's Lonely Heart's Club Band*, a marked departure from the popular music they had been making. The album is considered by many critics to be the best rock album of all time.

1969 The Woodstock Rock Festival opens in Bethel, New York, on August 15.

1973 Aerosmith releases their self-titled debut album, featuring the hit single "Dream On." This would lead to more than 30 years of success by the band.

1977 *Saturday Night Fever* opens in theaters; the punk rock group The Sex Pistols release their album *Never Mind the Bullocks, Here's the Sex Pistols*; Elvis Presley dies in his home in Memphis, Tennessee.

1981 MTV begins broadcasting on cable TV on August 1.

1982 Michael Jackson releases the album *Thriller*.

1983 Music is first recorded on compact discs.

1985 Live-Aid raises $70 million for African famine relief by filling stadiums in London and Philadelphia for rock concerts.

1991 Nirvana's second album, *Nevermind*, is released. It goes on to top many Album of the Year lists and receive much critical and commercial acclaim.

1993 Snoop Doggy Dog releases the album *Doggy Style*, which quickly becomes one of the most popular rap albums of the decade.

1998 Pearl Jam puts out their album *Yield*, from which their first video in several years, "Do the Evolution," is released.

2001 On September 21, a benefit for the victims of the World Trade Center terrorist attack of September 11 was held. Numerous celebrities volunteer their time to perform as well as answer the phones, while 89 million viewers watched across the country.

acoustic—in music, an instrument such as a guitar that produces sound without electrical amplification.

airwaves—the transmission, through the air, of radio and television signals.

amplify—to make louder; an amplifier projects the sound of an electric guitar or other instrument.

anthem—a song that becomes the symbol for a nation or a group of people with common beliefs.

blues—a style of music with roots in the black community. The lyrics often tell sad stories.

hodgepodge—result achieved by mixing different ingredients that don't share common qualities.

hysteria—uncontrollable outbursts of emotion.

LSD—drug that causes users to see and sense false images; the scientific name is lysergic acid diethylamide.

pompadour—a man's haircut that features a high wave near the forehead.

psychedelic—a distorted state of mind, brought on by drug use, often including deep feelings of happiness or sadness.

raunchy—tasteless and smutty.

reggae—music popular in Jamaica, often featuring lyrics intended to give hope to oppressed people.

rhythm—in music, the pattern or beats that gives a song its pace.

riffs—the notes played by a background musician to accompany a singer.

speakeasy—during the 1920s, clubs that illegally sold beer and liquor.

synthesizer—an electronic musical instrument that is capable of generating and modifying sounds electronically.

vocals—in music, the part of the song provided by the human voice.

FURTHER READING

Dister, Alain. *The Story of Rock: Smash Hits and Superstars*. New York: Harry N. Abrams, 1993.

Fast, Susan. *In the Houses of the Holy: Led Zepplin and the Power of Rock Music*. New York: Oxford University Press, 2001.

Shaughnessy, Mary Alice. *Les Paul, an American Original*. New York: William Morrow and Company Inc., 1993.

Sounes, Howard. *Down the Highway: The Life of Bob Dylan*. New York: Grove Press, 2001.

Szatmary, David P. *Rockin' in Time, a Social History of Rock-and-Roll*. Englewood Cliffs, New Jersey: Prentice Hall, 1991.

INTERNET RESOURCES

The Rock 'n' Roll Hall of Fame
http://www.rockhall.com/

History of Rock 'n' Roll
http://www.history-of-rock.com/
http://www.pbs.org/wgbh/pages/rocknroll/
http://www.legacylinks.com/
http://www.lifemag.com/Life/rocknroll/rocknroll.html
http://www.rocknrollvault.com/

American Bandstand
http://www.upenn/ccp/Ford/WPhila_AmerBandstand.html
http://www.geocities.com/Heartland/4547/clark.html

The Electric Guitar
http://www.angelfire.com/music2/myguitar/page2.html
http://www.gibson.com/products/gibson/Stories/LesPaul.html

PICTURE CREDITS

BARRY MORENO has been librarian and historian at the Ellis Island Immigration Museum and the Statue of Liberty National Monument since 1988. He is the author of *The Statue of Liberty Encyclopedia*, which was published by Simon and Schuster in October 2000. He is a native of Los Angeles, California. After graduation from California State University at Los Angeles, where he earned a degree in history, he joined the National Park Service as a seasonal park ranger at the Statue of Liberty; he eventually became the monument's librarian. In his spare time, Barry enjoys reading, writing, and studying foreign languages and grammar. His biography has been included in *Who's Who Among Hispanic Americans*, *The Directory of National Park Service Historians*, *Who's Who in America*, and *The Directory of American Scholars*.

HAL MARCOVITZ is a journalist for *The Morning Call*, a newspaper based in Allentown, Pennsylvania. He has written more than 20 books for young readers. He lives in Chalfont, Pennsylvania, with his wife, Gail, and their daughters, Ashley and Michelle.